A DECADE LOST

KIMBERLY WORTHINGTON FARMER

KWE PUBLISHING

Farmer, Kim Worthington. *A Decade Lost*
Copyright © 2024 by Kim Worthington Farmer all rights reserved.
ISBNs: 979-8-9905502-0-9 (paperback), (e-book) 979-8-9905502-1-6
Library of Congress Catalog Number: 2024909836

First Edition. All rights reserved. No portion of this book may be reproduced, stored in a retrieval system, or transmitted in any form or by any means - including but not limited to electronic, mechanical, digital, photocopy, recording, scanning, blogging or other - except for brief quotations in critical reviews, blogs, or articles, without the prior written permission of the publisher, KWE Publishing.

The information presented is the author's opinion and does not constitute any health or medical advice. The content of this book is for informational purposes only and is not intended to diagnose, treat, cure, or prevent any condition or disease.

Dedicated to my beloved son,
Travis Brantley Worthington,
February 26, 1993 - May 21, 2012

1

EVERY PARENT'S WORST NIGHTMARE

I believe that every parent's worst nightmare when they have children of driving age is to hear the phone ring in the middle of the night or hear a knock on the door at an ungodly hour because you know it is not going to be good news. I got that knock on my door in the early morning hours of May 21, 2012. My husband woke me up and told me that the police were at the door and that Travis, my nineteen-year-old son, had been in a car accident, and we needed to get to the hospital right away. I was confused, worried, and unsure of what I was just told because it was the middle of the night. I got dressed and went to the door, and the policeman was telling me that I needed to get to the hospital now.

I couldn't drive; I became numb.

"SEE, MOM? I AM INVINCIBLE"

I began thinking about last June when his friends came roaring through my front yard, running to the front door. They were saying, "Travis was just in a car accident on 460. You need to come with us now; it looks bad!" So I left my two children home with a stranger, one of my son's friends, without even thinking about it.

I went with his friend's dad, another stranger, to the crash site, not far from my home. And I saw the car and a helicopter. I stood on the side of the road, screaming, "Is he alive?"

By the looks of the car, I didn't think so, but luckily, he was. He only had whiplash, bruises, and scrapes. I felt a huge relief. I was also terrified.

The first thing he said to me was, "See, Mom? I am invincible!"

2

AT THE HOSPITAL

Back at my front door, I finally got myself together. The police officer and my husband had decided that I would ride to the hospital with the officer, and my husband would wait for a neighbor to come down to stay with our two younger children. It seemed like the ride took forever. It was a silent, lonely ride.

I called my mom and told her what had happened; she said she would meet me there. I kept thinking back to my conversations with Travis. Every time Travis would leave the house, I would say, "I love you, be careful," and he would say, "I will, I love you too, Mom. Nothing's gonna happen to me. I'm invincible." I would then say, "What's gonna happen to me if something happens to you?" His reply was always, "You won't be able to live without me." Here I was, thinking, *Is this it? Is this the time I have to live without him?*

When I finally got to the hospital, I don't even remember running in, but a nurse took me straight back to a holding room. All I remember hearing is someone saying, "They are working on him." I took that as a positive sign. My mom, husband, and sister got there. I remember calling my best friend, but I couldn't speak so the nurse spoke to her, and then she came.

This is where it all gets a little fuzzy for me, the order in which everything happened. I remember the nurse coming in, kneeling in front of me, taking my hands, and telling me that there was nothing more they could do for my son. I think I asked, "What do you mean?" I think she replied that he had suffered life-threatening injuries; he did not survive them. I remember lying down on the bed, just numb. I couldn't cry. I think this is the point I started to go into shock because I do have memories of some things that happened up until the next morning.

Everyone was crying. I remember looking at my husband, who is Travis' stepfather, and I have never seen him cry like that. The nurse was asking if I wanted to go in and see him, and I said no. My friend said she would go in and see him. She would tell me if she thought I should see him or not. When she came back, she was crying and she was very honest and said, "If he were my son, I wouldn't want to remember him like that. He is not bloody and scratched up; he just still has all the tubes and wires attached to him." Me, being a nurse, I knew what that meant so I decided not to see him.

I wanted to remember him the way I saw him that morning, smiling, hugging me, telling me he loved me and that he would see me later.

SHOES BY THE DOOR

When Travis turned sixteen and got his driver's license, car, and began driving on his own, I became a nervous wreck. I always told myself that I wasn't going to be one of those mothers who waited up until their child got home; that would drive me even crazier. So, Travis had a curfew while he was still in school, so he was home at a decent hour. The rule with him was that he had to leave his shoes by the door, so if I got up in the middle of the night, I would see his shoes by the front door and know he was home.

After he passed, I would still get up and look for his shoes by the front door, and when they were not there, I would just go to his room and cry. After several months of this, I got up one night, and a pair of his shoes were at the door. I was in disbelief and immediately ran to his room.

Later, I found out that my daughter had placed them there just so I wouldn't cry.

3

TRAVIS AND ME AGAINST THE WORLD

My parents divorced when I was eight years old, and when my mom re-remarried, we moved from Oklahoma to Virginia, away from my dad. My dad stayed involved as best as he could being so far away, and I visited him every summer, but I always felt something was missing in my life. I had a stepdad, but he was not involved in my life. I did not have a steady, present male role model in my life, so I looked for attention from boys.

My teen years were filled with failed relationships, boyfriends cheating on me, abusive relationships, and just an overall sense that I wasn't good enough and didn't deserve to be loved. These were my feelings, so when I found out that I was pregnant, I felt like I was finally going to have someone to love and love me back unconditionally. I was twenty-one and knew that I was going to be a single parent. At that time, his father did not want to be involved, but he eventually came around. I'm telling you all of this so you have an understanding of just how close and special my relationship with Travis was. It was just him and me for ten years. He was my everything. Everything I did, I did for him—to give him a better life, to give him everything he ever wanted. It was Travis and me against the world.

I was still living with my mom when I became pregnant with Travis and had no intentions of moving out. I had my career as an LPN, was making decent money, and she did not tell me that I had to move out. After Travis was born and I returned to work, working the 3-11 evening shift, I knew my baby was safe at home with my mom, so being twenty-two, I would go out with my friends and have a drink or two before going home. I took full advantage of my situation—and my mom. I did not realize this at the time, but it was pointed out to me later, when I grew up. I was not even helping her with any bills.

When Travis was fifteen months old, my mom came to me and told me that the lease was running out on our apartment and that she was moving. I said, "Where are we moving to?"

She replied, *"We* are not moving anywhere. I'm moving to a one-bedroom apartment."

I said, "What about Travis and me?"

She replied, "It's time for you to find your own place."

To this day, I jokingly say she kicked me out. This was the best thing she could have done for me.

CLOUDS

I was working full-time and going to school part-time, so I didn't have a lot of money to take Travis on vacations, so on my days off, I would try to make them special.

One thing Travis and I liked to do was take a blanket outside, lay on it in the grass, look up at the sky and clouds, and say what we saw. It was silly things like elephants, slices of pizza, anything, and we would just laugh. We would lay there for hours, it seemed, and just laugh and talk. It was our time to catch up.

This is ironic because ten years after he passed, I reconnected with an acquaintance, Mary Beth, whom I had met in passing several years before. I had come across her Facebook page and she had posted a video about her being a Soul-Shine Coach. I immediately reached out to her, and she remembered who I was but knew nothing about me. She had no idea that I had lost a child.

I booked a session with her, and in this session, Mary Beth asked Travis for a sign or symbol that he uses to show me that he is around, and he had her look up in the daytime sky. He showed her clouds, rainbows, and birds that got my attention. When she asked him, "How can your mom feel you?", he showed her the nighttime sky—looking up at the stars and the moon. He made her feel like the sky is his canvas to communicate with me. She has never heard a spirit explain their signs that way before; she says they usually only share one. I will share more stories of my sessions later in the book.

4

YOU DON'T PLAN FOR THIS

I don't know how long we were at the hospital; it seemed like a lifetime. The nurses would come in and check on us. The hospital chaplain came in. At some point, someone came in and asked me, "Where do you want us to send him?" I did not understand the question. *What are they asking me?* I think I told them, "Home." My husband said to me that they were talking about a funeral home. I just started crying. *How am I supposed to know?* You don't plan for this—why were they asking me this? At this point, my husband took over.

As we left the hospital, I still wasn't sure of what had just happened. I knew my son wasn't with us, and I knew I had two kids at home whom I needed to tell. What was I going to say to them? They were six and eight. How was I going to tell them? How was I going to help them through this? I didn't even know how I was going to survive this. I was going home from the hospital without him.

This isn't right, he is supposed to be in the car with us. We are going home, and he is not going to be in his room asleep, he is never going to be in his room asleep again. I'm never going to see his shoes by the front door letting me know he's home. I'm never going to see his car in the driveway. What am I going to do? I always told him I couldn't live without him. Why is this happening to me? This has to be a dream.

I don't know what time we got home. The next thing I remember is my mom waking me up, and I was relieved. I said to her, "I'm so glad you are here. I just had the worst nightmare ever that Travis died in a car accident." She started crying, and I knew right away that it was my worst nightmare come true. I began crying, and she stated that we needed to tell Brian and Austyn, my son and daughter.

Brian was six and Austyn was eight, and they were both very close to Travis. He was like a little dad to them. I did not know what to say, and to be quite honest, the conversation is a blur to me. I only know what I said because my daughter and mom told me later. My daughter said I woke her up with my mom and Brian and that I was crying.

"Travis was in a car accident last night," I said.

She and Brian both said, "Another one?"

I started crying even harder, and my daughter said at that point she knew it was serious. I then said to them, "He didn't survive this one."

They both started crying.

Everyone who has more than one child can understand what I'm about to say. You love each child equally but differently. I was grieving so hard for Travis that I admit that I had emotionally checked out. I was not there for my kids. I could not help them. I did not know how to help myself at the time. My relationship with Travis was so different from my relationships with Austyn and Brian. I had a husband with Austyn and Brian, someone who was there to help me raise them. Even though I was married, I felt like Travis was still only my responsibility. It was up to me to take care of him and protect him. It was that way for ten years; I could not just stop.

NO WEDDING DAY

I began thinking back to my wedding day. Travis walked me down the aisle. I realized, *I am never going to see my son get married.*

Suddenly, everything I was going to miss hit me. It was as if his future was flashing before my eyes, but it wasn't going to happen—he was gone. I'm never going to see him graduate college, have his first child, know what career path he would have chosen. I feel cheated.

He wasn't supposed to die before me. Parents are not supposed to bury their children; it is not the natural order of things. It is hard enough to think about losing your grandparents, and your mom and dad, but that is the natural order, I don't think anyone ever thinks about losing their child. It is the unimaginable.

Scott and I had prepared for his future. We had a college fund for him and our other kids. We did what parents do—try to make them self-sufficient so they would be successful in the world when they get out in it. He was robbed, just like everyone who knew and loved him and the people he was going to meet.

5

IT'S NOT MINE

Everything from this point on has been told to me; I don't remember any of it. We had to go to the funeral home that day to get the obituary done, pick out a rental casket because I was having him cremated but wanted a viewing, and pick out an urn. I have no time frame for the events. I just know there were a lot of people at my house all the time, a lot of phone calls, and a lot of family members flew in from Oklahoma—some I don't even remember being there to this day.

I think it was the day before the viewing ceremony that we went to the funeral home to view his body. I was told that when I saw him, I fainted. I don't remember seeing him then, at the viewing, or at his funeral. I don't remember my son's funeral. Sometimes, I wish I did; other days, I'm glad that I don't.

A couple of months after Travis died, my mom was over and helping me out, and I was doing laundry. There was a pair of pants and a shirt that had been in the laundry room for a while, and I did not know whose it was, so I never washed it. My mom handed it to me, and I told her, "It's not mine."

She said, "These are your clothes. This is what you wore to Travis' funeral."

I said, "I have never seen those. They are not mine."

She then explained to me that my cousin, Melissa, had been here and that she had gone shopping and bought me that outfit to wear. I was dumbfounded. I didn't even know Melissa was here.

I started asking my mom, "Who got me ready? Who did my hair and make-up?"

She told me that I did. I don't remember anything.

A SPOT OF TEA AND FROZEN PEAS

Travis would come into my room if my husband was working the night shift and wake me up by saying, in his made-up British accent, "Mother, would you like to get up and have a spot of tea with me?" It would make me laugh so hard; he was such a goofball.

Recently, I was flying on British Airways to Italy, and the flight attendant came by. She was British and asked, "Would you like a spot of tea?

I immediately started crying, and she began apologizing, not knowing what for. I told her, "I'm okay, you did nothing wrong. And no, thank you, just water." I'm sure she thought I was crazy.

It's little moments like this that get me.

* * *

I remember several years after he had passed, and I was in the grocery store in the frozen food aisle. I came across the frozen peas, and I started laughing and crying at the same time. I know people around me thought I was crazy, but I remembered a time when he was in elementary school.

I was at work and the nurse called me. She began telling me that Travis was playing kickball and that the ball had hit him between the legs, and he wanted to come home. Travis got on the phone, and I asked him, "Are you okay?"

He says, "Not really, my nuts hurt. The nurse gave me ice but it's not really helping, can you come get me?"

I'm laughing, trying not to let him know, and explaining to him that school is almost over and that I will be there soon. He then says, "Do we have any ice packs at home?"

I replied, "I don't think so."

He says, "Okay then, just go by the store and get a bag of frozen peas so I can put them on my nuts when you get home. We don't eat them, anyways."

He was so funny. I miss that.

6

THE FIRST YEAR IS THE WORST

After a funeral, everyone leaves and gets back to their normal lives. You are now left alone, and you can't move on. Nothing is normal. Your entire world has just been turned upside down, and you don't know what to do. I was a single parent with Travis for ten years. His father was involved, and we were not together, but I found comfort in talking to him as he reminded me of Travis. Travis had a lot of his mannerisms, and he looked like his dad. He was very comforting to me, and I needed him in my life. He made me a mother for the first time; he gave me Travis. I loved him for that, and I love him to this day for that. Unfortunately, because of some decisions that I made after Travis passed, before I received help, his father and I are no longer in contact with each other. I hope that one day that changes. I would love to be friends with him again. Travis loved him so much, and they had so much fun together. They would play paintball and fish, and his father introduced him to hockey, which Travis played and loved. Though we were not together, he was very involved in his life.

Travis' father was an amazing father to Travis, as his whole family was amazing. His dad had an older brother, who had two sons, and an older sister, who had three daughters. Travis was actually born on his cousin Caroline's birthday two years later. He spent every other weekend with his dad, and the majority of the time, his cousins were there. Every summer, his dad's family went to the beach for a week, and they would rent a big beach house and all stay together.

Travis loved the beach. He was a Pisces, and he loved the water. He would surf and skimboard—there was nothing he was not good at. That was Travis' favorite way to spend time with his dad and his family. On the weekends, he was with his dad. They would go fishing, play with airsoft guns, and play hockey. His grandfather lived on a big farm, and he and his father would just stay outside and do all sorts of things. Travis loved going there.

* * *

Every time I talk to people, especially mothers who have just lost a child, I usually tell them that the first year is the worst. The first year is experiencing all the holidays without their child and the first birthday without their child, but I'm going to stop telling them this. At the time of writing this sentence, I just had the eleven-year anniversary without my son, and I have to say, every year gets harder for me. It's been eleven years since I've seen his smile, heard his voice, or felt his hug and kiss. It's going to be a long time until I see him again, so I miss him more and more every year. The pain softens, but the yearning grows deeper.

I think about the fact that I could be here for another forty years, and that is such a long time without him. I find myself jealous of my relatives that pass because they get to see him.

It's funny how some people are still so uncomfortable talking about Travis with me. When I bring him up in a story, their whole body language changes. It's like they are afraid I'm going to break down. I can talk about my son without crying. I love talking about Travis and telling stories about him; it is healing for me. I want people to know him. He was an amazing person, and I want the world to know what they missed out on. I hope this book shows everyone what kind of person my son was, how special our relationship was, and how important he was to his sister, brother, and his father.

COMPLICATED GRIEF

I really didn't know if I was going to make it that first year without him. Looking back now, it seems like such a whirlwind of time. Where did it go? I guess I would call it going through the motions of "living." I was afraid to smile. *How dare I show happiness. I was afraid to laugh, have fun, God forbid, my son just died. I'm not happy, I'm not supposed to have fun. If I do any of these things, it means I'm not sad anymore, it means I'm over grieving the death of my son, but I will never get over the death of my son. Will I ever be happy again? I have so much guilt when I want to laugh. What am I supposed to do?*

This is how I lived for two and a half years. I tortured myself with guilt. Like I said before, I was seeing a therapist, but I was stuck in a cycle of complicated grief, which means an ongoing state of mourning that keeps you from healing. Signs and symptoms are intense sorrow, pain, and rumination over the loss, focus on little else but your loved one's death, problems accepting the death, numbness or detachment, isolation from others, deep sadness, guilt, and self-blame and feel life isn't worth living. I had all of these symptoms. This is what led to me being placed in the treatment facility. Travis would not have wanted me to be living like this, and I realized that after treatment.

7

FISH OUT OF WATER

After a few months, I reached out to a therapist. I was desperate, I was suicidal, and all I wanted to do was to be with Travis. I was so angry at God for taking my son that I wanted to take my own life. In my mind, that would show Him. I was not being rational, but at the time, it made sense to me. How was I going to live without him? Stephanie, my therapist, was the only therapist who called me back after I left desperate messages for several therapists, I think it was on a weekend. My message stated through tears that I was suicidal, and she saw me that day. I have been with her for the last eleven years, and now, I just call her when I need her. There were days that I just sat in her office and cried the whole hour. I was a broken woman and saw no light at the end of my tunnel.

I describe myself as a fish out of water that first year. It took everything I had to breathe and get up in the morning. It was like I was learning how to live again—except I didn't want to.

That first Christmas, I did not want to be at home, so we flew to California and had Christmas with my family out there. Somehow, I thought if I wasn't home, Christmas wouldn't come. I had my mom come to my house and set up Christmas for my kids so I didn't have to do it. She set up the Christmas tree and wrapped the gifts.

Christmas was always a very special time for Travis and me. When I was a kid, before my parents divorced, I remember coming downstairs, and I could barely see the carpet. There were so many presents. I wanted this for Travis. Granted, my dad was a dentist, and I was a single parent barely making ends meet, but I made it happen.

One Christmas—I think Travis was four or five—after he opened all of his gifts and I was lying on the couch, he came up to me and asked, "Are you Santa?"

I replied, "What do you believe?"

He said, "I believe there has to be a Santa because you can't afford all this stuff."

I laughed so hard, and he was so serious. This is one of my favorite memories.

BIG BROTHER

As I'll explain later, Travis had asked for a sister or a puppy for his fifth birthday, and of course, at that time, he got the puppy. Well, five years later, Scott and I found out that we were pregnant with a girl. When we told Travis, he was so excited to be a big brother. He talked about how protective he was going to be and how she wasn't going to date until she was twenty-eight, and he was going to tell her all about yucky boys. Remember, he was ten at this time. When she was born, he was immediately like a little dad to her. He would get up in the mornings before I did and get her up and make her a bottle. He never would change a diaper, but he did everything else, and she loved him right back. Their connection was immediate and deep.

When I became pregnant with Brian, Travis was again excited. He looked forward to having a little brother to teach all of his "chick secrets" to. He also wanted to teach him to look out for his sister. One of the most important things to Travis was making sure that Austyn was protected by any means necessary. He wanted Brian to know and understand that, but unfortunately, he never got the chance to share that.

Travis loved his siblings, and they loved him. They truly missed out on having an amazing big brother for advice and guidance.

8

"YOU SHOULD BE OVER THIS"

After a year and a half, I was seeing my therapist weekly but not making any progress. I started drinking more than I used to, and my husband started working a lot of overtime. He is a mechanic, and all he knows how to do is fix things; he wanted to fix me, but I was unfixable. So, he started working a lot of overtime just to avoid coming home. He did not know how to be there for me emotionally. I know my friends were getting tired of hearing me cry over losing Travis, too.

At this same time, two of my closest friends told me they didn't know how to be my friends anymore. They were the two people who had been there for me since day one. We had been talking about planning a trip together with our families, so I was over at one of their houses one day, and they began talking about the trip. I said, "Have you all decided on a date?" They replied with, "Yes, but it is just us that are going. It's been a year and a half, and you should be over this by now. We don't know how to be your friend anymore."

I was devastated! They were the only two people that I had left so in my mind, I was all alone, I now had nobody to talk to. I had other friends, but I had isolated myself from them. I really felt I had nobody to turn to. I couldn't turn to family close to me because they did not know what I was going through. They said they did, but they did not. They would call to ask me how I was, and I would say, "Not good." They would reply, "I'm not, either. I know exactly how you feel, I lost Travis, too." I understand my whole family lost Travis and what a huge impact it had on everyone, but they didn't lose their child, their firstborn son. They still had their children. I hope they never truly understand how it feels.

Before Travis died, I was very social. My friends and I would get together very frequently to hang out at the pool, go to concerts, meet for lunch or dinner, and around the holidays, we would get together and have parties. I was always doing something with somebody. After he died and my friends said they didn't know how to be my friend anymore, I thought that I was a burden to everyone, so I just quit calling people. If a friend did call, I might answer the phone, I might not. If I did answer and they invited me somewhere, I would make an excuse not to go. I didn't want to be seen in public for the risk of running into someone who knew what had happened. I also didn't want to risk seeing somebody I had not seen in a while who didn't know what had happened and would ask about Travis.

It was a year after he had passed, and I received a message through Messenger from one of Travis' friends from junior high who had moved back to Peru after eighth grade. He and Travis had lost contact. He had been looking Travis up on Facebook and saw that he had passed away. He sent me a long message, asking me if it was real. He was in disbelief. I had to tell him what had happened. This is what I wanted to avoid in public face-to-face.

At this point, I had nobody. I was not upfront with my therapist, or anyone, about how much I was drinking, though my mom knew. She would tell me, "You are not going to find

Travis at the bottom of a wine bottle." I didn't care. It numbed the pain for a while.

As I sit here now, eleven years later, looking back on that first year after Travis died, if I could visit myself, I would say, "You are going to survive this. You are going to have some very bad days, but that's okay. Don't give up; lean on your friends and family. I know you feel alone, but you are not. Be honest with yourself, your therapist, and your husband. They can't help you if you're not."

Knowing what I know now, I would have done things differently. I would have included my children in everything instead of sending them to the neighbor's house. I would have tried my best to be there for them and help them through their grief.

REGINA'S STORY

I met Kim I think in 1999. We worked together at Westport Convalescent, a nursing home, where Kim was the charge nurse on wing one. I became a licensed practical nurse in 2000, and Kim became my preceptor. We clicked instantly! Our friendship flourished. We started hanging out with each other and attending each other's family events. Her family has always been so welcoming.

We often discussed our family dynamics, her being a single mom to Travis and me being in an interracial marriage with little family support. I valued Kim's advice. Kim is white, and I am Black, so she gave me her "white" perspective of issues, and I gave her mine from the "Black" perspective. And her opinions were refreshing but ONLY shared between us! She was always honest and gave me insight on "the other side" of the issue. We could confide in each other about ANYTHING! That's why we worked.

When I was pregnant with my daughter, I prayed that I would have the same maternal instincts as Kim. I remember Kim would start Christmas shopping for Travis in July to make sure that she was able to afford all that Travis wanted. Everyone at work knew how hard she worked to provide for him—so much so that she decided to go back to nursing school full-time while working full-time. She changed her work schedule, sometimes working the evening shift or even every weekend.

On the day that Travis died, I was working. Kim and I had stopped working together, but we kept in contact. I am not quite sure of how my husband found out about Travis' death. I don't know if he saw the accident coverage or what, but he called my best friend and told her to tell me because he was not sure of how I would handle it. Once I was told, I was completely numb. I called Kim several times with no answer. I called Laurie, a former co-worker of both of ours, and she told me the details of the accident. I got off work and went to Disputanta, where Kim lives. I saw Kim. I hugged her, and we sobbed. My friend was inconsolable. Understandable. Crushing. I so wanted to make everything all right. I felt helpless. All the time, questioning death and God. Why take Travis, Lord?

I spent the night at Kim's house. She did try to rest that night. I fell asleep on the leather sofa in the open living room. I awoke in the middle of the night with an image of Travis standing in front of me. Maybe it was a dream. He was wearing a white button-down canvas shirt and a pair of blue jeans. There was a golden aura around him. He didn't speak. He just stood there. Surprisingly, I wasn't scared. I felt a sense of calmness, kind of like a reassurance that he was in a better place.

The next weeks after the funeral were a blur. Kim's mood and behavior worried me. She was eating very little, drinking a lot, and not sleeping or resting. At times, she would burst into tears and then display no emotion. Fearing that she wasn't staying hydrated, I kept asking, "Did you pee?"

I found this grievance group that was held every Thursday at 6 p.m. in the old church. We attended for about a month. She shared a little. Not much. She continued to drink. She would call me when she was drinking, stating that she did not know how she would live without Travis. I would say, "You must think about Austyn and Brian." She wouldn't respond. There were just tears.

I remember her telling me about an incident at the beach that happened while she was on vacation with her family. She said, "Regina, I walked out into the water so far from the shore. I wanted to leave. I wanted the water to just take me, cover me, so that I could be with him."

Her marriage suffered. She started seeing another person. I often was her cover-up. We were the cover-up for each other. We both were going through issues in our marriages. I was willing to do anything that would possibly return Kim back to Kim. I thought Kim would take her own life.

I thank God that today Kim is KIM! I don't expect her to be the same person she was before Travis' death. No person is after a devastating loss. But she is no longer stuck living IN grief. She is enjoying life now, traveling a lot, spending time with family, and even working again. She even created a Facebook page in memory of Travis. Kim will never be KIM completely. Grief is constant. There is no time limit, and there should be no expectation of "getting over" it. The presence is always there. To hear her laugh and to see her smile again says to me that my buddy is resilient. I understand that pieces of her were lost, but her soul is here. And I am SO grateful that she is.

9

LOOKING FOR A SAFE PLACE

I hurt my husband by having an affair. He was not there for me emotionally. He wanted to fix me, but he couldn't, so he started working long hours at work just to not come home. He did not understand what I was going through and the pain that I was in. Travis was his stepson, so he couldn't imagine my pain. I don't blame him for this. It's just how it was. Since I felt that I was alone, I started looking for someone to talk to that was completely unrelated to my situation. I wanted to escape my reality for just a little while. You see, I was still at the point where I was unable and unwilling to accept the fact that my son was gone and never coming back. That was too painful to accept, and I was just not ready.

I looked up an old boyfriend of mine, whom I had been in touch with over the years. He had met Travis when he was one year old. I found out that he lived near where I was seeing a chiropractor, so one night, after my appointment, I stopped by his house. When he saw me, he hugged me. It was a long, tight hug, and I just fell apart. That's what I had been needing for so long. Someone to hold me up and make me feel secure. I didn't go looking to have an affair. I knew he was an alcoholic, so his house was a safe place where I could drink without judgment. We would just drink, watch movies, and talk about the past. It was easy and comfortable; it was my escape, a whole different world. It eventually turned into more.

My husband found out and forgave me because he knew that that was not who I was. Under normal circumstances, that would have never happened. He came to me one day and confronted me and just said, "I know you are having an affair, and I forgive you."

Of course, I still denied it, but I knew he knew. I don't think that I really ever came out and openly admitted to it until I was in an inpatient facility. He was at the facility, visiting for family therapy, and I had to explain to him why I had the affair. I began by telling him that it had nothing to do with him. I didn't do it to hurt him, though it did. It was all about me and not wanting to live in reality and accept the fact that Travis was gone. I was escaping it. I was looking for a safe place to get away from that had no reminders of Travis and had nothing to do with my life.

After my husband found out about my affair and exactly how much I was drinking—and that I had actually hit rock bottom, meaning that I had been contemplating suicide since my son had passed—my therapist, mother, and husband got together. They thought it would be a good idea for me to go to an inpatient facility. They decided this behind my back.

My husband, kids, and I were planning a vacation for the end of July 2014. I was actually looking forward to it. Before we left, we had a session with my therapist, and I was told then that after vacation, I wasn't coming home. I was being dropped off at a facility for intense therapy for my complicated grief, and I would be there for a month. I was angry. I felt ambushed and blindsided. I did not see this coming. Vacation ruined!

Needless to say, the vacation was great, and the facility I

went to saved my life. I had been living in denial, not wanting to accept that my son was never coming home, so two weeks into my stay at this facility, I was in a session with a therapist who practiced and taught mindfulness. She was trying so hard to get me to say out loud that Travis was gone and he wasn't coming back. After a while, I finally yelled it through tears. Have you ever seen the movie *Ghost* with Patrick Swayze and Whoopi Goldberg? There is a scene in the movie where Patrick's character enters Whoopi's body so he can hold Demi Moore's character. All of a sudden, she was, as I call it, "being whooshed" out of her body, and she falls into a chair. This is what happened to me in this session. After I yelled, "Travis is gone, and he is not coming back!", I had my *Ghost* moment!

I fell back into the beanbag chair and felt a huge weight being lifted off of me, almost like something left the room. It was so freeing. That was the turning point in my healing process. After two and half years of intense grieving, I was finally able to accept the fact that my son was gone and that I had two beautiful children who still needed me and a husband who needed me and still wanted me after all I had put him through. I was finally healing. Now, it was time to go home and deal with the real world.

This was also a very scary time for my husband and me. I was now back at home after my infidelity and was unsure of what to expect. I didn't want to talk about it, but I knew he didn't trust me, so I had to start earning his trust back. I think for the first month, I didn't go anywhere except to take the kids back and forth to school. After that, if I needed to go to the store, I would call and ask him permission or tell him exactly where I was going. This went on for about a year, and every now and then, he would bring up the affair. I let it go; I felt he had every right to do so.

As time went on, two or three years later, he would still bring it up, and it would anger me. I understood that I had hurt him, but he had also said that he forgave me—but I knew he had not forgotten. I told him that the only way we could move past this was to stop throwing it up in my face. I had owned up to my mistake, I had apologized profusely, and I had worked so hard at forgiving myself that I could not be reminded randomly about what I had done. We eventually got past this, and we have a better, stronger marriage because of it.

LAURIE'S STORY

I've known Kim for over twenty years. We met when I landed a job at a skilled rehab facility. I was placed on the unit where Kim had already been working. We were the two main nurses on that unit and became not only co-workers but friends as well. What drew me to Kim was her compassion and dedication toward her patients and also the fact that she was a single mom raising a six-year-old boy. That boy was named Travis. All of the staff at the facility got to know Travis as Kim enjoyed sharing pictures and stories and an occasional visit on her day off. We became her work family and looked forward to watching Travis grow.

Kim eventually got married and had two more children. She had made the decision to quit her job and become a stay-at-home mom to raise her children and give them the best life possible. Kim and I remained friends; we kept in contact and got together whenever we could. She was my go-to confidant when I was having problems. Even though she was a busy mom, she never hesitated to be there for me.

I remember the day I learned of Travis' tragic passing. I was at work, and a co-worker told me that he had died in a car accident. Immediately, my thoughts turned to Kim, and I tried reaching out to her. It took a while before she returned my calls, and she confirmed the news. Travis had a car accident and had passed away from his injuries. She was inconsolable as she told me what had happened. All I could do was listen to her, grieve with her, and let her know I was there for her.

The funeral was emotionally devastating for everyone. We as her work family were there to support her, and we all saw her falling apart. I wished I could have done something more. All I had were my hugs, hoping they were enough but feeling that they weren't.

After a few years had gone by, I learned that Kim had been admitted to a treatment facility to help her cope with her loss. She phoned me after she had been released, and we made plans to get together. I could tell from her voice that she was broken, disconnected, and just hanging on. Over the next few months, we tried to continue our friendship. I began to realize it was going to be a long and difficult journey. I guess maybe I was selfishly putting my own needs first, expecting and needing our relationship to be as it was before. Kim had always been there for me, the voice of reason, compassion, and love. She was the only person who never judged or got upset with me. She was by my side through some of the most difficult times in my life, and now, she needed me to do the same for her.

I felt inadequate as a friend because I wasn't sure how to deal with this new version of Kim. When we would see each other or speak on the phone, it was as if she wasn't engaged in our conversation. She was a shell of the person I once knew. I understood her thoughts were with Travis, but at the same time, I felt frustrated. I needed her, and she needed me, but neither one of us was able to fulfill our obligations as friends, so I made the difficult decision to step away for a while. I thought that would give us both time to heal—her from the loss of a child, me from the loss of a friend.

Today, Kim and I are back on track. I couldn't imagine not having her in my life. I know a piece of her will always be missing, but the attributes that connected us initially are still present—compassion, dedication, and understanding.

What I've learned from this is that nothing is promised in life. People change, and situations change.

10

EVERY TIME

People who had not lost a child would tell me they knew what I was going through, they knew how I felt, and they felt the same way. It would really upset me. How could they know? They still had their children. Every time I came home, it was a reminder that I was missing a child. I had a fully furnished bedroom with clothes, and the bed was never going to be slept in by Travis again. I had all his favorite foods that were not going to be eaten, I had a laundry basket full of his clothes that I didn't know what to do with. Every time I pulled into my driveway, I would look for his car and would always realize that I would never see it again. It was the constant daily reminders that I had to remind me that he was gone and never coming back. I was living in hell. What was the point of getting up every morning? What did I have to look forward to?

In reality, people really don't know what to say to you, and that is fine. Sometimes, they shouldn't say anything at all. I had one friend tell me that she had just lost her dog, so she knew how I felt. Others would say that it was God's will, that He needed him more than I did, that God had a bigger plan, and I would understand when I got there. I know that people meant well, but over time, these comments would just piss me off. They did not know what I was going through! None of them had lost a child! I had people tell me that I was not the only mother in the world who had lost a child and that I needed to get myself together. My reply would be, "I know I'm not the only mother who has lost a child, but right now, I lost *my* child!"

AMANDA'S STORY

The experience of losing a loved one was not new to me when Kim called that fateful morning in 2012. Like many other people in my age group, I had lost grandparents, great aunts and uncles, and elderly neighbors. Of course, it's always sad when a person who is important to you passes away after living a long, fulfilled life of love and many experiences. But it's easy to know what to say to your friends when their ninety-year-old grandfather battles dementia and passes away in his sleep. When your friend calls to tell you their nineteen-year-old son was gone after a terrible car accident? No one prepares you for that.

When I met Kim at a local preschool where both of our middle children were attending, I felt an instant connection to her in a way that I hadn't with anyone else in a very long time. She and I both have a bit of a standoffish persona (me more so than her) until we're comfortable enough to open up. While I don't remember our initial conversation, I do remember that we were suddenly fast friends and began to grab coffee, have play dates, and swap stories about our husbands and kids—Kim with her three, Travis, Austyn, and

Brian, and me with my three, Braxton, Camden, and Dawson.

Having three boys myself, my oldest being six years younger than Travis, there were many times I complained about "boy" things to Kim since she had been through it, and was going through it, with Travis. She helped me through a lot of times when I wanted to pull out my hair because my kids were making me insane.

As we became closer friends, she shared with me many stories about her being a single parent and raising Travis. Their connection was palpable through her words. She had a bond with him that was very unique. She wanted his life to be nothing short of special, and her actions as a single mom helped prove that. While I do not know what it's like to be a single parent, there has always been a small part of me that held a piece of jealousy for the type of relationship that she and Travis had in his early childhood. Having one-on-one time with a child in that way has to create such a magical sense of love and commitment, even during difficult times.

I got to know Travis through the stories Kim told me. And when I spoke with him at their house or at birthday parties, I'm sure he had no idea that I knew all of his dirty little secrets from childhood. And I know he would have been thrilled! But he was always so nice and polite. His love for Austyn and Brian was evident—he adored them.

As the years went by, Kim and I remained good friends. We traveled together several times prior to Travis' death—both on girls' trips and with our families—and we continued to come and go in and out of each other's lives while everyday, mundane life went on. Our friendship has always been the type where we can go for quite a while without speaking and then pick right back up where we left off like not a day has passed. Months could have gone by without contact, and if something major happened in my life, the first friend I would call was Kim. When Travis had a car accident on the last day of school in 2011, she called me. We kept in touch for the important things, and I always knew Kim was there if I needed her—and I hoped she knew the same about me.

I was standing in the kitchen when my house phone rang, and Kim's number popped up on the caller ID. I picked up the phone and stood in the living room listening to Kim's voice. Her tone was out of character. Sleepy. Exhausted. "Travis was in an accident last night." In my head, I immediately thought about the previous phone call when she had called to tell me about his car accident. *Oh, no, not again.* After a quick pause, she said through heavy tears, "He died."

This entire scenario is burned into my brain, and I remember it like it was yesterday. I told Kim some niceties like "I'm so sorry. Oh my God. This is horrible. Oh my God. I'm sorry." And then, within thirty seconds to a minute, the phone call was over, and I was standing there in disbelief. What I felt is really beyond words. It was like pure emptiness. Nothing. No emotion. No breathing. No vision. No thinking. Absolutely nothing. It was like a powerful force had pushed gravity on me so that I could not move. This lasted for a solid two to three minutes. And then the emotions kicked in, and I lost it.

After I got myself together and started processing what was happening, I canceled an interview I had with a prospective employee, wrapped up my stuff for work and pretty much checked out the rest of the day. I was mentally exhausted and knew that if I was going to do anything to help Kim, I had to get myself in a better place first.

At this time, Kim had several other close friends who I knew would be taking control of all the dreaded funeral procedures. She had her mom and her sister as well. I knew she was in good hands and didn't need me specifically to do anything. I wanted to be helpful in some way, but I really didn't know what to do. Again, no one tells you what to do in a case like this. The following morning, I had to get involved and not sit back. So I drove to her house just to be present and be with her.

The house was somber and quiet, except for Fonzi, her dog—my nemesis (thankfully, I grew to love him and his licks). There were lots of teenagers and several of Kim's friends and family. Kim appeared to be in a state of shock, out of it, glassy-eyed, but somewhat jovial in a sad way. This day was meant to celebrate Travis' life with his closest friends and family around. And that's exactly what we did. There were photo albums and stories and memories. Kim was so proud of a Mother's Day card that Travis had given her just weeks before. I think she showed it to me at least three times.

While there were a lot of happy memories being shared, the tears streaming down faces and looks of worry could not be overlooked. The sadness was unlike anything I'd ever seen —you could feel it, as if it was another person in the room you could wrap your arms around. Seeing the pain of Travis' friends was extremely difficult for me. Their tears made me think of my own kids going through something similar. So yes, I commiserated with Kim as a mom, and I felt her pain the best that I could, but I also felt the pain of those kids for losing their young friend.

In the days ahead, I would spend much time at Kim's house. When everyone went to the funeral home for a meeting, I stayed behind with Austyn and Brian, and we played games and watched TV. It was cathartic to just be silly and play with them during such an emotionally traumatizing time. Brian's giggles when I made *Toy Story*'s Woody say, "Howdy, howdy, howdy!" made me smile and forget why I was there.

A week after Travis' death, Kim's house had started to become quieter. Her out-of-state family had left. Most of her friends had gone back to work. Travis' friends had gone back to their daily lives. I was more concerned about the weeks and months ahead than I was the previous week. The quiet was going to be rough for her and the family. One morning, when I arrived, I saw Scott outside on my way into the house, and I said, "I know everyone has been checking in on Kim, but how are YOU doing?" Scott, being the quiet, humble guy that he is, said, "Good." I told him to make sure he was taking care of himself and eating well so that he could take care of Kim.

I spent many hours sitting beside Kim in her bedroom while she zoned out, cried, and told me how much she wanted her son back. I listened to her tell me how much she missed him, loved him, and needed him. There are only so many times you can say, "I'm sorry. I can't imagine how you feel. I'm so sorry," before it starts to sound disingenuous. But this is all that I could really say. I have never done very well with trying to console people when they're sad. I feel awkward and uncomfortable. This brought my discomfort to a whole new level. I felt terrible thinking about myself, though; my discomfort did not compare to hers. I should have been concerned for my friend and not worried about my own feelings. So I just continued to listen and be present.

Days turned into months, and Kim was still going through the motions of grief and mourning. She was a shell of the person she once was. She would call me and check in, and the conversation would quickly turn to sadness about Travis. I found myself at a loss for words once again, but I kept listening and trying to do what I could to steer the conversation to lighter things whenever possible. I would ask about Brian and Austyn, talk about my own kids, and always try to keep a smile on my face while we talked so I could at least try to seem happy while we chatted. I stopped asking, "How are you?" because that was a painful question that never led anywhere good. I tried my best never to slip up and say, "I know how you feel," instead saying, "I cannot imagine," or "I know you must feel terrible."

I didn't know how Kim felt. I didn't know what she was going through. I only knew what it looked like from this side of the trauma—not from the first-person vantage point. And from this side? It was bad enough. When I said, "I cannot imagine," I truly meant that. Her pain for Travis was almost identical to her love for Travis. Immense. Intense. Immeasurable. I know that type of love, having three children of my own. I can only hope I never have to experience that same level of pain. So, no, I didn't know how Kim felt, and I didn't understand what her new normal was like. But I needed her to know that she was being heard.

The next few years are a bit of a blur with our friendship. Life went on. We still checked in on each other occasionally, but it was different—a little more distant, a little less in-depth. I wanted to know how she was doing, but I knew the answer already. Even when we went for months without talking, I thought about her often and worried if she was okay. I knew she needed her space and that this was her way of processing her grief. I continued to text and tell her, "I'm here when you need me." I had no idea what was really going on in her life outside of the quick phone calls here and there. There really was no discussion about anything deep, just superficial conversations about nothing or talks about her grief. Kim distanced herself not just by lack of communication but also by withholding what was happening in her life. And I went along with it because I thought this was just part of the process.

Kim called me one day to tell me they were taking a vacation to Smith Mountain Lake and that she was not coming home but going to a facility immediately after the trip. I was stumped. I had no idea what that was about. What the hell was going on that brought this about? What had happened in the last two-plus years that my friend needed rehab? I felt terrible for not being present enough to know what was happening and if there was something I could have done to prevent this. I was confused, concerned, embarrassed, and mad at myself. It wasn't until she returned that I would find out the answers.

It was September, and Kim had invited me for coffee at our old stomping grounds from our mom of preschooler days. I hadn't seen her in person in months. When she walked in, I was pleasantly surprised to see what appeared to be the version of Kim that I remembered from years ago. She looked different. Her eyes were brighter, her body language was cheery, and she was smiling. I could just feel her presence was the complete polar opposite of what it was the last time I'd seen her. She was a new Kim. While not exactly the same Kim as years prior, this new Kim was comfortable in her new normal. The transformation was unexpected, and I could not have been happier for her.

We talked. And talked. And she laid out everything that had occurred in the last few years since she had pulled away. I was shocked by much of what she told me, but I knew she was in a much better place now, and all of that didn't matter anymore. From there, we worked on rebuilding our friendship that was always there, just a little bit broken. We repaired our connection, and I got to know the new Kim and how to be there for her in a way that I was unsure about previously. She needed me to listen, hear her, and not be afraid to talk about Travis. That's what I've done ever since.

Today, our friendship is stronger than ever. She gets me and deals with my constant sarcasm. I know her traumatic past and what triggers to avoid. Knowing her story has helped me be a better friend in the present day. Looking back on when Travis' death consumed Kim's entire life, I wish I knew then what I know now. Simple things like being present, listening, don't listen just to reply, speak, or share. Just listen. Be patient. When hell comes to town, you don't know how long it's going to be here. Have patience, and let your friend do what they need to get through their trauma. Just be there for when they come back around. And when your friendship starts to rebuild, be accepting of the fact that your friend is a new version of themselves. Do not try to change that.

11

LIKE NO TIME HAD PASSED

I was very nervous about going home. It was the weekend before school started, so I knew that I was going to be home alone the following week. Before leaving the facility, I had to have a plan in place for therapy and other activities to keep me busy. That weekend, my husband and I took the kids to Busch Gardens and just spent the weekend having family fun and reconnecting. I also needed to reconnect with my friends, the ones who I knew were my true friends, the ones who left me messages randomly that just said, "Thinking about you." Amanda was one of them. We had been friends for many years before Travis passed, and she was with me after Travis passed. Over time, I had stopped calling her and isolated myself from her and others. When I did reach back out, it was like no time had passed, and we picked up where we had left off. She knew I was different but accepted me for who I was now. She didn't bombard me with questions about where I had been, what the facility was like, how I was feeling now, and if I thought it worked. She just let me talk about what I wanted to, and she listened. I wanted to know about her and her family, and when I was ready, I would talk about what I had been through.

When you go through something like this, you find out who your true friends are. They are the ones who you haven't talked to for months, but when you finally pick up that phone, they say, "I'm so glad you called. I've been waiting for you."

I have several true friends besides Amanda—Regina, Donna, and Laurie, to name a few. If I didn't name you, you know who you are.

SECRET CLUB

I didn't share with everyone at first that I had gone away to the treatment facility. Not that I was ashamed, but I just needed time to adjust. I needed time to forgive myself and continue healing, and I had to take a good look at the people who were in my life. I had to cut out the toxic people. To me, the toxic people were the ones who said they knew what I was going through, saying though they had not lost a child, they felt like they did. It's not the same. They could not be there for me. I could not talk to them, so I had to cut them out.

It's strange how many people come to you and tell you their story about losing their child after you lose yours. I had two neighbors come to me and tell me about the children they lost. I had no idea. It's like it's a secret club, and they become the only people you feel comfortable talking to because they truly understand.

12

THREE TATTOOS, ONE ANGEL

Since Travis has passed, I have gotten three tattoos. I said in the past that I would never get a tattoo, but I felt the need after he passed. The first one I got is on the outside of my right ankle, and it is just his name with his date of birth over his name and his date of death below his name with some red hearts. I got that several months after he passed. I was already in so much pain, so I thought, *How bad could it hurt?* Well, it hurt really bad! That is a very sensitive area. The second tattoo I got is on the outside of my left ankle, and I got that one when I came out of the inpatient facility I was in. It is very meaningful to me because I was on my journey of healing, and I felt that I wasn't broken anymore, so the tattoo says, "Broken No More" with red hearts. I had an idea for my last tattoo, but I was unsure if it existed. I wanted it to be a rhythm strip of his heartbeat, but I didn't know if he had one that night.

It was coming up on ten years since he had passed, and I knew that after ten years, hospitals destroy medical records. I decided one morning that I was going to go to the hospital and request his records. When I got there and put the request in for them, the clerk at the hospital handed me a piece of paper. I asked her if that was it, and she said yes. I explained to her that it was for my son who had passed away there on May 21, 2012, and I wanted all of his records from that night. She called someone, and a little while later, another woman came into the room and handed me a CD. She told me that it was a copy of his chest X-ray. I was devastated at this point. I waited too long, and now, I would never know if he had a heartbeat that night. I left in tears.

As I was driving home, I decided I needed some comfort food, and I wanted nachos. I knew I had tortilla chips at home, but I felt the need to stop and get more, so I stopped at a local store to get some. I went in, only taking twenty dollars with me, and they did not have a single bag of tortilla chips. So, I walked around, looking for other comfort food, and I decided on ice cream. I got three small cartons for myself and the kids and picked up several other things. Then, I went to check out. I realized that I only had a twenty on me and that I had probably more than twenty dollars' worth of stuff, so I let the two gentlemen behind me go ahead so I could go get more money out of my car.

When I came back in, it was my turn, and this lady at the self-checkout started talking to me, trying to give me a coupon. She was saying that she came here every Saturday to buy five candles so she could use her coupon, and she was going to give me one. I declined, and we said our goodbyes.

When I exited the store, the woman approached me near my car and said, "You look sad."

I replied, "I just got some bad news, but I'm okay."

She then said, "I lost my nine-year-old several years ago."

I was a bit caught off guard but said, "I'm so sorry."

She then asked if she could hug me because she said I looked like I needed a hug, and then I just lost it. I told her that I had also lost a son. We talked for a bit, but she was very vague in her responses. When I asked her where she lived, she replied, "Around here." And when I asked her if she was on Facebook, she replied, "I will find you," but we never exchanged names.

We hugged several times, and then I got in my car. I have this thing hanging from my rearview mirror that says, "Sometimes I just look up and say, 'I know that was you, thank you.'" Well, that was just swinging away for no reason, and I looked around, and I was the only car in the parking lot. There was no sign of this woman.

I sat there for a moment, confused, so I went back inside the store and asked the clerk if she had ever seen that woman before. She replied, "What woman?" I then explained to her the one who was at the self-checkout and trying to give me a coupon. She then said to me, "We were the only ones in the store."

I know the look on my face was probably of complete and utter shock, so I had her look at the store video and the parking lot video. In the video, it was only the store clerk and me! In the parking lot, it showed me getting into my car, sitting there for a minute, getting out, going back in, then coming back out and leaving. There was no woman! Travis sent me an angel that day! He knew I needed one to give me comfort.

When I got home, I immediately told my kids what had happened, and my son was skeptical at first, but this really happened. I saw it with my own two eyes. There was proof on the video recording. So needless to say, my third tattoo is not of my son's heartbeat.

Years later, I was cleaning out my closet, and I found the last Mother's Day card he gave me. He died a week after Mother's Day, so I took the card to a tattoo shop, and they transferred what he wrote in the card to my left wrist. It is his handwriting, and it says, "I love you Mom, Love, Travis." It is a very special tattoo to me—more special than his heartbeat, so as they say, everything happens for a reason.

PERMANENTLY DIMMED

After Travis died, I didn't share this with many people, if anyone, but I was so angry at him. He knew I couldn't live without him, and now he was gone. Then, I felt so guilty for being mad at him because he wasn't there to argue with me, to tell his side of the story. So, I got angry at God. I felt like He gave me this precious child nineteen years ago for a reason, to make me grow up, become more responsible, for whatever reason, so why the hell did He take him from me at the age of nineteen?

I'm telling you all of these things because this is how my story went, and I don't want anyone else to make the same mistakes that I made. Also, my deceased son has played a huge role in my healing process.

People who knew me before he passed tell me that I have a look of sadness in my eyes, that they don't shine as bright as they used to. That's because a part of me is missing and I will never get it back, the light is permanently dimmed.

13

ALL DAY, EVERY DAY

I hurt a lot of people within the first two and a half years of my son's passing. I was hurting, and the people closest to me were collateral damage—the first being my kids and Scott, my husband. I was there physically for my kids but not emotionally. I didn't know how to be. I couldn't help myself, and I certainly couldn't help them. Travis died in May of 2012, and I went back to work in September 2012 as I was a one-to-one nurse at my kids' school.

I thought going back to work would be good for me, having a daily routine, being around people again, and being in a classroom with children. I was so wrong. I soon realized that I didn't have any patience for the children because everything they did really annoyed me. And every time I walked down the hall, people who saw me and knew what had happened would stop me and say, "I'm so sorry for your loss. How are you?" Then, they would hug me, and I would instantly break down. This happened all day every day.

All I wanted was to be treated like normal, and even when people wouldn't say anything, they would walk past and give me a head-tilt look with a frowning-face look. I knew the moment Travis died that my world would never be the same, but I didn't expect the world to treat me any differently. Looking back, what I wish people would have done when they saw me was just smile at me and say, "It's so good to see you," or "You look great; glad to see you back at work." I just wanted normalcy so I could make it through the day.

TRAVIS' ROOM

Coming home also meant that I had to deal with Travis' bedroom and seeing all of his stuff just as he left it. He had always said that when he moved out, he wanted Austyn to have his room because his room was big, almost the size of the master. I don't remember how long it was after I came home that I went into his room and started boxing up his belongings to prepare the room for Austyn, but I did. I did not throw anything away, though. I put everything in boxes and containers and put them all in the closet of Austyn's old bedroom. I took the sheets, pillowcases, and comforter off of his bed, stuffed them in a container, and put a lid on it. I wanted to trap his smell in the container. This was very difficult but also therapeutic as his room used to be a place for me to run and hide after he passed. It became kind of like a shrine, and it was not healthy for me. We let Austyn pick out new carpet and paint and moved her in, and she brought new life to the room.

14

PINK CLOUD

They say after therapy that you are on what's called "the pink cloud." You are happy, and everything is good—until it isn't. You eventually come down off of this high, but if you really learn how to use your new tools in therapy, you will be okay. I learned how to use my tools. I started meditating. This is a wonderful tool to have. When my mind would start racing, I would make myself stop thinking and just go meditate. I had so many apps on my phone that I would just randomly pick one to get me through the moment. I made time for my grief. I also started practicing mindfulness. This is a hard one, and it takes practice. This is a practice of being present and sitting with your pain, letting yourself feel the pain, and working through it. I use this to this day.

Before I can reach out to friends or strangers who have lost a child, I must re-live my pain through mindfulness so I can better help them. If I don't, I can very easily get so wrapped up in their pain, which is detrimental to my well-being.

* * *

I had my son cremated, and I have his ashes at home on a dresser in my room. The box looks like a jewelry box; you wouldn't know what it was unless you asked me. I did that because he still lived at home, and to me, he's home. When I say I make time for my grief, for me, it is a time when I'm alone and I'm able to talk to Travis. I tell him how I'm feeling, how much I miss him, thank him for giving me a sign, or I just simply sit and cry. This is important because you will grieve forever; you just need to make time for it. We talk about Travis all the time. It keeps him alive for us. He had such a huge personality that it is hard to tell a story and not mention him.

I wanted to start doing something positive with my grief. I wanted to help other mothers who have just lost a child. I wanted to let them know that they were not alone and that I knew what they were going through. I wanted to offer guidance about what was to come in the days and weeks ahead and to be someone they could talk to who understood and would listen to them cry. In one of my sessions with Mary Beth, she told me that Travis showed her an image of him in spirit helping others. She wasn't quite sure what he was trying to say, so she asked him to be more specific. He explained that he helps children cross over by explaining what's happened and helps them acclimate to the spirit world. It was amazing to hear and to know that he is helping the children while I am helping the mothers. He was always kind like that.

"YOU WILL UNDERSTAND WHEN YOU GET HERE"

I think about Travis every minute of every day. I feel sorry for the people who missed the chance to know him, I feel sorry for the people who did know him because I know how much they miss his presence. He was such a vibrant person, so full of life, so charismatic. He would walk into a room and just light it up with his smile and laughter. I hate the fact that his little brother and sister have had to grow up without his guidance and that his cousins, Alex and Brooke, missed out on having him as they grew up. They were very close. He loved spending time with Alex and Brooke. Alex was three years younger than him, and Brooke was five years younger. They spent a lot of time together. Travis even went to Disney World twice with them.

My family and the world lost an amazing young man who had his whole future ahead of him, and yes, it sometimes still makes me angry. This was told to me by Mary Beth in one of our sessions by Travis, "You will understand when you get here."

15

HOW THE MIND WORKS

It's funny how the mind works. I don't remember the two weeks following the accident. I have snippets of memory, but they are so vague. What is clear to me is the accident itself. I never saw the police report, and I never asked questions about where it happened. I never heard anyone talk about it; I didn't want to know anything about it. I felt like I knew I would never drive on that road. I would dream about the accident very vividly, but it wasn't my son in the car. It was his car, but he wasn't in it. I would wake up and ask my husband questions about the accident, and he wanted to know how I knew certain things.

Over time, I had recreated the entire accident in my mind down to the exact spot where it happened. I can't explain how, but for four years, I avoided that road completely. When my daughter started eighth grade, I had to start driving down that road because that's where her school was. I was a nervous wreck. I didn't know how I was going to handle it. I did know that the tree he hit had been cut down, so there were no markers. I do wish that I had known when they cut the tree down so I could have at least gotten a piece of the tree just to have.

After my son died, his friend put a cross on the tree and made a memorial at the site where he crashed. I understand why they did it, but when I found out about it, I asked them to take it down. I did not want to memorialize the site on the side of a road where my son died alone. I knew that one day, I would have to drive past it, and I did not want to see a constant reminder of where my son died. They understood and respectfully took it down.

As we were driving down the road and getting closer to the site, I began crying uncontrollably and did the only thing I could think of—I turned the radio up really loud, thinking it would drown out the noise in my head. It worked! I was shaking, crying, and full of anxiety, but I did it. My daughter thought it was great, so from that day on, every time we passed it, we turned the radio up really loud.

Some time had passed. I was asleep, and I had the feeling of someone watching me. I opened my eyes, and there was my son, floating above me. He was just smiling at me. Again, it was just a few seconds, and he blew me a kiss. Then, he was gone. I remember thinking to myself, *If I can continue seeing him like this, I think I will be okay.*

Several months later, it was the middle of the night. We have a king-size bed, and this particular night, both kids ended up in our bed. I woke up and was hot, crowded, and uncomfortable, so I got up. I usually got up and went to my son's room to sleep, but that night, I went to my daughter's room. As I lay in her bed with my back towards the door, I heard footsteps going down the hall to my son's room, and someone turned on the light in his room and then turned it off. Then, the footsteps came toward my daughter's room. Someone turned on the lights in her room where I was, and I heard, "What are you doing in here?"

I replied, "I couldn't sleep."

He came and laid behind me and put his arm around me. At this time, I wore my son's class ring on a chain around my neck. He touched the ring and said, "Why are you sleeping with this on? It could choke you or break."

I said, "I don't want to take it off."

We lay there for a few minutes. He hugged me tightly, kissed me on the cheek, and said, "I love you."

"I love you, too," I said.

He got up, left, and turned off the light.

The next morning, I got up to wake my husband up for work, and when I walked into the bedroom, he said to me, "Where have you been?"

I said, "I was in Austyn's room. You knew that; you came in there last night."

He said, "No, I didn't, I didn't move all night."

I explained to him what had happened, and he said it wasn't him. About that time, my daughter woke up, glowing, grinning from ear to ear, and said, "Mommy, I saw Travis last night! He took my hand and took me to heaven! It was so beautiful! He came to you, too; do you remember?"

All I could do was cry. My son was helping me.

When I was young, I was made to go to church, so as an adult, I chose not to go. I am a Christian, and I believe in God, but I don't believe that you have to go to church to be a believer. I do believe that my son is in heaven, and I believe he has shown me heaven in my dreams. When I dream about Travis, the dreams are so vivid.

The time that I believe he showed me heaven, I was standing in a field full of bright-colored flowers that I could see for miles. There were rolling hills of the greenest grass that I have ever seen. I remember just standing there with a warm sensation on my face, and when I turned around, Travis was standing there. I asked him where we were, and he just smiled and took my hand. He never spoke; he just led me around. We walked around for hours, it seemed, and then my childhood dog, Pretzel, joined us. He was so happy and free, just running around and jumping. Travis showed me all the animals, tigers, bears, and giraffes just to name a few. He then turned to me, gave me a huge hug, and kissed me on the cheek.

As he walked away, I began crying. I woke up, and I was crying, touching my cheek. I could smell him. I felt his arms around me. This was real; this had just happened. My son took me to heaven. I have had many dreams about Travis, and he never speaks in them, but when I wake up, I always feel his presence.

It is hard for me to put a timetable on the first time that he visited me after he passed. I know the first time was soon after he had passed, and I think he was just letting me know that he was okay. It was sometime in the middle of the night, and I heard wind blowing loudly. I could tell there was a bright light, so I opened my eyes, and there standing in the doorway of my bedroom was my son. He was glowing, waving, and smiling at me. I reached out for him, he blew me a kiss and he was gone. I knew it wasn't a dream because I was wide awake. All I could do was cry and say thank you. I was sad yet comforted at the same time.

THERE IS NO GUIDE

I realize now the damage I caused my kids by not being there for them, and I have apologized and am doing my best to help them now. I made a lot of mistakes, and I own them. There is no guide on what to do when you lose a child suddenly. I did the best I could with what I had, and I am stronger for it.

My daughter, at eight years old, felt like she had to be strong for me. When I found this out, my heart broke for her. I then became angry at myself for not noticing this after I got help. I did feel like I failed her for not allowing her to grieve the loss of her brother. She came to me one day, I think she was around twelve or thirteen, and just simply said to me, "I think I need help." I'm thinking about homework, but she says, "With a therapist, someone to talk to."

I responded, "Okay, about?"

And this is where she told me how she felt like she needed to be strong for me at the time Travis passed and that she had never grieved the loss of him. I can't tell you the shame, guilt, heartbreak, and utter hatred I felt for myself at this moment. My daughter, who was very close to her big brother, had been suffering in silence because of me! She did not want to upset me, so she kept quiet about her own feelings. I just hugged her and cried and apologized, understanding that my words would never be enough to make up for the pain I, her mother, have caused her. At this point, I still felt like I failed Travis for not protecting him. Now, to find this out was devastating. I immediately called around and found a therapist who could see her as soon as possible and she started on antidepressants and therapy.

Today, she is thriving. She graduated high school and became a dental assistant and loves what she does. She knows that Travis is looking down on her and smiling, he is very proud of her, and in one of my sessions with Mary Beth, Travis acknowledged that she had a boyfriend and that he was a good kid. Then, he joked that if he was earth-side, he'd give him a hard time to not break her heart, but in a loving, big brother way.

16

THIS WOUND NEVER HEALS

I have dealt with grief in the past when my granddad passed away and when my father-in-law passed away, but this was different—this was a pain I had never felt before. This was gut-wrenching, heart-stopping, can't-breathe, dropping-to-your-knees kind of pain. And the stages of grief—denial, anger, bargaining, depression, and acceptance—don't go in order. I still go through anger and depression. Grief is a journey, and it is a personal one. There is no time frame for it, and you will never get over losing your child. It is not the natural order of how things should go. People always say that time heals all wounds, but this statement is not correct for this situation. This wound never heals. You have a permanent hole in your heart, a piece missing. You carried this child in your womb for nine months, loved it, protected it, and then gave birth to it, and for some reason, no matter how much time you had with this child, he/she is suddenly gone. You can't get over that.

Throughout the years since Travis has been gone, I have made new memories without him, but I also include him. Every year for his birthday, he wanted everyone to get together to go to his favorite restaurant, Kanpai, for dinner.

We did, and we still do. I always take cheesecake because he didn't like traditional birthday cakes, and we celebrate him every year.

One of my favorite memories was on his fifth birthday. I kept asking him what he wanted, so one day, he came to me and very seriously said, "Mom, I know what I want for my birthday. Since I'm turning five, I believe I'm responsible enough to have one of these two things. I want a sister or a puppy." He was so serious that I tried not to laugh. Needless to say, he got the puppy that year.

On the anniversary of his death, we go to his favorite place, Belle Isle on the James River, and we throw roses in the river for how many years he has been gone. This May, it will be twelve. For Christmas, I still hang his stocking every year. It would seem wrong not to. I also order a Hallmark in memory ornament for him. Ironically, every year since he passed the ornament has been a seashell, and he loved the beach. I just think that is so cool.

Facebook has been a great tool for me as well. I started a page called Mothers Who Have Lost a Child, and through this page, mothers from all over reach out to me—some with questions, some for support, and some just needing someone to talk to. It has been very therapeutic for me. Facebook also lets me keep up with Travis' friends so I can see how they are doing. Sometimes, it makes me sad, like when I see them getting married and having children. I'm happy for them but sad for me, knowing what I have missed out on.

* * *

I have mentioned Mary Beth, a medium I've seen several times after Travis's passing, so now I will share more of what she has shared with me through my son. The first time that I connected with her, as soon as Travis showed up, he showed her sneakers, a purple pair. I had to laugh because Travis loved shoes! He would buy a new pair, and when he would put them on to show me, he would walk all stiff-legged and say, "Do you like my new shoes?"

I would laugh and say, "Yes, but why are you walking that way?"

His reply was always, "I don't want to crease them."

Today, I have a bag of brand-new shoes that he never wore because he did not want to crease them!

He then showed Mary Beth a series of items like someone having a memory box for him, and then a blanket and a body piercing. Austyn has all of these. Travis made a blanket when he was in school, and she sleeps with it.

In my second session with Mary Beth, Travis seemed to be more focused on my health. He was adamant that she share with me to stay on top of my routine testing and screenings, like mammograms and bloodwork. Then, there was an acknowledgment of my heart chakra needing to be opened and balanced. I wasn't sure what that meant, so I made an appointment with a cardiologist and found out that I have a leaky heart valve. It's nothing serious, but it needs to be monitored. I was also overdue for my mammogram, so I scheduled that, and what do you know, I was called back for an ultrasound for something suspicious. It turned out to be nothing, but Travis led me to these tests through Mary Beth.

Mary Beth has brought me so much peace and comfort. Her gift is truly a blessing, and she does it with such dignity and grace. I thank God for putting her in my life.

STEPHANIE'S STORY

As a therapist, the primary goal is to assist a client through a healing journey to come out on the other side as close to their old baseline or finding and accepting a new personal baseline or healthy level of functioning. This, of course, is different for everyone as they learn to navigate the impacts of emotional pain and trauma. It is not easy and it never goes away but with hard work, perseverance, and the practice of new skills it is possible. This is what I experienced with Kim.

When I met Kim, she was a shell of a person due to the death of her son. Kim and I worked slowly over the next several months just to restore her ability to believe that she would be able to live without Travis. There were times when she wanted to give up but was able to dig deep to carry on if only in that moment day by day living for her other children and family. During darker times for Kim, treatment felt like it was standing still as some sessions were used simply as a safe space to vent about the future she would not have with her son as she looked toward upcoming birthdays or holidays. Those sessions were necessary and productive from a treatment standpoint as they slowly allowed her to start to establish her new normal. Although painful, she was establishing what her new life without her son would look like. Kim also struggled with guilt of how consumed she felt by Travis' loss and the impact her being emotionally absent was having on her family.

We worked on filling her "emotional toolbox" with skills to manage her depression, anxiety, and grief, including learning mindfulness, emotional regulation, and distress tolerance skills. Just like with any new skill, it takes practice on a daily basis so that when those overwhelming emotions or ruminating thoughts start to creep in these skills can be easily accessed. Through the therapeutic process, Kim was able to accept that she would forever have a new normal and she could go on with Travis. Kim was able to do the hard work necessary to be a mindful, loving, supportive, and present parent to her two living children and husband. Kim accepted that she was not stuck and did not have to struggle through her grief alone. Kim did the hard work necessary to come out on the other side of this devastating, life-changing event, reclaiming her new sense of self and reclaiming her mental health.

"TRAVIS DID IT"

So many things have happened around the house that can only be explained by "Travis did it." Travis was a jokester. He liked to prank people, and he did it to my dad the year he died at the beginning of college football season. My dad lives in Norman, Oklahoma, and we have been lifelong OU Sooner fans. It is to the point that my dad does not allow any of us to wear orange because that is a Texas Longhorn color, and they are OU's rivals.

I got a phone call from my dad one day, and he said, "Your son is haunting me from beyond."

All I could say was, "What did he do?"

He explained to me that he has a plant on his patio that blooms pink flowers every year and that when he and Carole went out to water it. Two orange flowers had bloomed instead. All I could do was laugh. That is so Travis.

Today, I still grieve the loss of my son, and I always will. He was my firstborn, and we had an unbelievable bond. I talk to him every day. I always look at the sky to look for signs. Every time there is a rainbow, I take a picture of it.

We have what I call a tree in our front yard; my husband calls it a very large weed that looks like a tree. In the fall and winter, it is very ugly, but in the spring and summer, it starts to bloom, and every year, a cardinal arrives. The cardinal is a sign that our loved ones are always with us. Every year, my husband threatens to cut the tree down, but I will not let him.

My kids are grown and doing well now. Of course, they miss Travis, but we have learned how to live a new normal. We have pictures of Travis all over the house, and we talk about him all the time. Like I said before, grief is a never-ending journey. You will have good days and bad days, and as time goes on, the good days will outweigh the bad. In the beginning, this seems un-survivable, but with great support of family and friends and a great therapist, you will survive and find out just how strong you really are.

17

THE NEXT THING I KNOW

Sunday, May 20, 2012. It's late in the morning, and I'm in my room, folding clothes. Travis comes into my room and tells me he's leaving to go down to the James River. He and his friends always hang out at Belle Isle. He hugs me and tells me he loves me. I tell him that I love him too and to be careful and check in with me later. He leaves.

Around 7:30 that evening, he called me from a number that I didn't recognize. He explains to me that he is at Haley's house, his girlfriend, and that this is her phone number because he lost his phone again. If I need him, call her number. He says he will be home in a little while and that he will let me know when he gets home. I tell him to be careful because it might rain.

He says, "I will, Mom. I love you."

I say, "I love you, too, Travis."

We hung up.

The next thing I know, the police are at my door.

ACKNOWLEDGMENTS

I would like to dedicate this book to several people. First and foremost, to my beloved son, Travis Brantley Worthington, February 26, 1993–May 21, 2012. You were my firstborn. You taught me what it was like to love unconditionally and what it was like to be loved unconditionally. I only had you for nineteen years, but they were the happiest and best nineteen years of my life, and I wouldn't trade them for anything. Even knowing how things ended, I would do it all over again. I love you more and more as each year passes, and I know that I will see you again one day. I will never stop missing you.

Next, I want to dedicate this book to Travis' father. Without him, I would not have had Travis. You gave me my firstborn son, and for that, I am forever grateful. I love you for giving me such a wonderful son. I know how much you loved him, and I know how he loved you. I hope one day we can reconnect and talk about our son together and remember the good times that we had with him.

Of course, I also dedicate this book to my husband, Scott, and my children, Austyn and Brian. Scott, you stood by me through the worst time of my life. I put you through hell, and your love for me never wavered. I am so thankful for you and the love that we share. Through this tragedy, we have grown stronger together, and I can't imagine my life without you. Austyn and Brian, the two of you give me hope for the future. I lost hope for a long while, and I hurt both of you in the process, and I am sorry for that. Travis loved you both so much, and he is watching out for you from above. Thank you for not giving up on me. I love both of you so much.

I would like to thank Stephanie. You were there for me from the beginning. You helped me find the light at the end of my tunnel when I didn't think it would ever be possible. I can't ever thank you enough.

Mary Beth, our paths crossed for a reason many years ago, and I am so thankful that they did. Words can't express how much your gift has helped me. Through you, I can stay connected to my beloved son Travis. Thank you from the bottom of my heart.

I want to thank Amanda for sharing her story for my book. I know I did not make it easy on you those first couple of years, but you never left my side; even when I left yours, you were there when I came back and needed you. I am so grateful for our friendship, not just because you take me to Disney, though that is a perk, you are a true friend. I don't know what I would do without you in my life. I do love you.

Thank you, Regina. What can I say, you have always been there for me as well. We come from two different worlds, but somehow that is what makes our friendship so special. You are the one person I can ask about anything when it comes to racial issues in the world and can debate them without judgment. Though we don't talk to each other all the time, we know each other is there when we need each other. You make me laugh so hard my stomach hurts when I get off the phone with you. Stay true to yourself, never change. I love you and thank you for sharing your story for my book.

Laurie, our friendship has been like a very long roller coaster ride, full of ups and downs. Sometimes, I wanted to jump off, but I never did, just hit pause. We are in each other's lives for a reason, for better or for worse, and I love the fact that I never know what is next with us. What I do know is that it is always interesting, entertaining, and fun. I can't imagine you not being in my life. Thank you for being a part my story. I do love you.

ABOUT THE AUTHOR

My name is Kimberly Worthington Farmer and I live in Disputanta, Virginia. I am originally from Oklahoma; that is where the majority of my family is and where I consider home. I have a loving husband of twenty-one years, Scott, and two wonderful children, Austyn, who is twenty, and Brian who is eighteen, whom Travis loved so much, and they loved him back. The last twelve years without Travis have been challenging as a family. Without the support of my mom, Charlie King, sister, Sharra McKesson, father, Brant Worthington, and stepmom, Carole Worthington, this journey would have been impossible. We, as a family, have survived, and as a mother, I have survived the unimaginable —the loss of a child. I hope this book helps mothers, friends of mothers, and anyone else who has suffered a tragic loss. That is my purpose and why I wrote this book.

ABOUT THE COVER DESIGNER

I would like to thank my niece, Brooke McKesson, for the absolutely fabulous book cover design and illustration. When I asked her if she would design the cover for my book, she was humbled. She was afraid that she would not be able to come up with a cover that captured "the essence" of who Travis was. I had complete faith in her because she knew him, she knew how special he was, and she knew his humor, his personality, she knew what he loved. She knows what signs are important to me—rainbows, cardinals. She knows what was important to him—shoes, surfing, the beach, and catching waves. This book, I have poured my heart and soul into it. My niece, who lives in Tampa, Florida, so all this has been done by texting and FaceTiming, has struggled, but in the end, she captured the true essence of Travis Brantley Worthington, her cousin, my son, in this amazing book cover. I am so thankful and honored that she did this for me without hesitation—a little trepidation, but WOW! I love you so much! Thank you!

ABOUT MARY BETH THOMSEN, SOUL SHINES COACHING

Mary Beth Thomsen, owner of Soul Shines Coaching, who helped me a lot in this process as mentioned throughout the book, is a psychic medium. She is also a Certified Master Color Energy Coach and a Certified Spiritual Life Coach. She has the ability to hear and see messages from the divine —some call it the Universe, angels, spirits, our own intuition, or Higher Self.

Mary Beth is both a clairvoyant and clairaudient—this means that she is an energetic conduit for receiving guidance about you, and for you, through seeing and hearing. In client sessions, she will call upon your angels, guides, and loved ones in spirit.

She offers intuitive guidance sessions, mediumship readings, or a combination of both. She begins the session by setting the intention for messages to come through for your best and highest good, to clear and ground her own energy, and share a brief prayer to connect with you on a soul level. Mary Beth will channel information to help you grow mentally, emotionally, and spiritually.

Clients often say she makes them feel safe, supported, and seen.

For clients who would like to work together on a longer-term basis, she also offers a life coaching program. Mary Beth uses a variety of modalities to help clients proactively elevate their personal or professional lives. She helps with accountability, clarifying goals and identifying strategies to meet those goals, and uncovering limiting beliefs.